Contents

Introduction

Religious turmoil, peasant revolts, and infant states

Judicial State measures

The diversity of the persecuted beliefs and conducts

Early Modern skepticism and Renaissance Humanism

Decisive developments towards ending the witch hunts

Conclusion

Notes

Introduction

The massive witch hunts in the 16th and 17th century belongs to the category of phenomena in European history which have been subject to grave misunderstandings and scientific disputes among the respective agents within several disciplines, such as history, folkloristic and social anthropology. However, it is only in the later decades that scientific research has gone through an upsurge regarding the issues related to the witch hunts, for instance through deeper investigations into local historical source material such as judicial and fief administration records. These studies have provided far more insight into the quantitative dimensions of the persecutions themselves, as well as a broader understanding of the very content of the beliefs allegedly subscribed to by these socially marginalized and persecuted people in the early modern era. As regards the origins of the phenomenon, however, and its eventual fading away by the end of the 17th century, there remains a lot to be said – and certainly disagreement to be had. For quite some time there were allegations which insinuated that *millions* of people were victims of the witch hunts in Europe's early modern period. However, new research has revealed that the number approximated 60 000, and that their most intensive period overlapped with challenges towards the infant states of the period in the form of peasant tax rebellions and military disobedience. It will be seen, from the perspective of the present author, that an extent approximating millions of witch processes would simply have been counterproductive to the very intent of the state persecutions, by the simple fact that it would have instigated more rebellions than it would have been able to quell: In the highly tumultuous period when the witch hunts took off – the post-reformation era – the modern European states was still in their infancy and continually faced with politically disintegrating, decentralizing, and even confederal, countercurrents; hence, the ruling elites of the respective crowns retorted to the universal Machiavellian strategy of *divide and conquer*. So, the fact that the actual number of persecutions was far lower than once thought – and the number of acquitted suspects generally amounting to 50 % -- does not diminish the importance of the phenomenon; quite to the contrary, both facts served the purposes of the state very well indeed. The all too simple way of jumping into historical conclusions by way of mere *numerical* and *quantitative* data, does no good for our understanding of important developments in history. The human *psyche* is hardly measurable in any quantitative way, and the disruptive social effects of the very fear of "diabolism", slander, and state persecution surely demands much more of the researcher than "counting heads".

As regards the very content of the beliefs which were fiercely attacked by the authorities, there is today common consent among researchers that it consisted in a combination of *demonology*, developed as a theological discipline in the late 15th century – as manifested in the infamous *Witch Hammer* (*Malleus Maleficarum*) published in 1486, and written by the Dominican monks Heinrich Kramer and Jacob Spränger – and ancient, local superstition and tribal religion. Hence, in the first century after the reformation most people – especially in the Northern parts of Europe – clung to the time honored Catholic beliefs, mixed up with ancient folklore, so that virtually every commoner was a potential victim of witch persecutions, although women (75 %) came to be worst hit; a fact that comes naturally if only by the simple tenet within demonology that witchcraft entailed "a date with the devil" – a date with explicit sexual overtones at that – and hence constituted an implicit threat against the hegemony of patriarchy, which had become increasingly more predominant within the reformed ideology which had done away with the worship of Virgin Mary. The Catholic faith was not hurriedly buried anywhere in Europe, and was quite persistent in the north, a fact that fits well with the notion that the witch hunts were intimately connected with the ideological needs of the state, which manifested and anchored its power in exactly the time period which corresponds with the end of the witch hunts, which will be seen below. Firstly, however, we must take a look at the political and economical background of the persecutions, which reached their height in the late 16th and early 17th century. In this context it will also be necessary to consider the importance, in the actual period, of the contest between two ideological and politically organizational principles and manifestations: The confederally structured, and highly prosperous, United Dutch Provinces, accompanied by the thrifty and harmonious Swiss confederation on the one hand, and the autarchic and centralized states of France on the other – with England and Prussia somewhere in between. In the early 17th century, the "future was wide open" and there were no guarantees as to which ideology and political orientation would prove victorious or even hegemonic. Moreover, however much the radical and anti-authoritarian heretics of the Middle Ages were defeated militarily, their legacy lingered on all the way into the modern revolutionary era – somehow as a ghost of the radical clerics Thomas Münzer and Wilhelm Pfeiffer and their huge armies of co-rebels during the German Peasant Wars in 1524-25.[1]

Religious turmoil, peasant revolts, and infant states

In the honor of human progress – however incomplete – which is intended to be a main focus throughout this book, the emphasis in this essay is put on the fading away of the witch hunts towards the end of the 17th century. In considering the reasons why the witch hunts ended relatively abruptly in this time period, however, it is obviously of some interest to direct attention to the origins of this phenomenon, which eventually was to flourish for a reasonably limited time span, compared to other more lasting religiously related phenomena. As already indicated the witch hunts was to an overwhelming extent a post-reformation phenomenon – although they originated in the border regions between France, Italy and Switzerland[2] as soon as the Medieval heretic movements were defeated, by the mid 15th century, during the birth of the modern state – and reached its most widespread extent in protestant countries, such as the Scandinavian ones. For the countries in the North, the developments in the German states from the time of the mass publication of Kramer and Spränger's *Malleus Malificarum* and throughout the tempestuous years of protestant reformation until the Peace of Augsburg in 1555, became of major importance. It is tempting to infer that had communications between German and Scandinavian peasants somehow been better in that era, the monarchs and fiefs of the latter countries would have had to deal with far more threatening peasant revolts than those which actually occurred, even if the northerners were generally considerably better off politically, if not necessarily economically, than their German brethren, among whom feudal structures were far more deep seated at the time of the Reformation. On the other hand, the fact that the tales of the tremendous

German peasants' struggle could only reach their class fellows in Denmark, Norway and Sweden in the form of *legends*, months and years after the events, could also in its peculiar way encourage the spirit of the Northern peasants. Indeed, the spread of information in the form of such legends would tend to tone down the hard facts about the ultimate defeat of Münzer, Pfeiffer and their numerous collaborators. Moreover, the threat posed by these peasant insurgents was not lessened by the clerical background of their leaders, such as Münzer, who was accused of "Anabaptist communism" by the aristocratic elite. Thus, according to historian and philosopher, Murray Bookchin:

"In the German speaking areas of the Holy Roman Empire, many ideological factors – the Reformation and its radical offspring – came into play that seemed to challenge the authority of the ruling elites and that gave a strong cultural edge to peasants' economic demands."[3]

The very tendency in the Reformation struggle towards demands of a more just world, fanning the claims of the commoners, was soon countered by the jurisdiction of the state authorities, who usurped whatever vestiges may have remained of the time honored *peasant legalism* of the Germanic world. The new Mosaic Law, for example, introduced in Denmark-Norway not only strengthened the state's jurisdiction at the cost of the clergy and its old Canonic Law, but vastly extended the state's claim to power over the individual. The infant states' need, not least in Northern Europe, for enhancing its judicial power – in the decades following the German peasants' War – was accentuated by the tendencies among the revolutionary German peasants, and their allies in cities over vast territories in Germany, to form decision making bodies of their own during the revolutionary upheaval in 1524-25. Moreover, at this point the states were militarily weak – all over the continent – with the possible exception of the Iberian Peninsula. Avoiding the trap of reading history backwards, one easily recognizes the importance of fact that, at this crucial turning point in Western Civilization, the confederated Dutch Provinces were about to rise to prominence (with Antwerp becoming the financial centre of Europe), the Swiss confederacy flourished as never before in its neat balance between town and country, underpinned by democratic structures based on popular assemblies, and the Scandinavian peasants fraternizing across the borders in times of war between the dynasties frenetically trying to impose discipline among their subjects – all of which were powerful currents rendering the new born institutions of the state highly precarious. To the extent that internecine tensions were marginal, there was doubtless a palpable need for "enemies within" for every one of the courtly powers, in their determined urge to eradicate popular movements leaning towards a confederal and anti-authoritarian orientation. In fact, so strong was the peasants' power – at least periodically – that German dukes called themselves "peasants" in order to gain their allegiance, as exemplified by the Duke of Württemberg, who took the name "Utz the Peasant" (!)

As the peasant revolts in the Scandinavian countries about the time when Luther published his "theses", in 1517, were largely non-affected by the religious strife, and more motivated by efforts to retain their freedoms inherited from the past against the influx of feudal tendencies by way of German fiefs appointed by the Danish and Swedish courts, the state administrations readily turned the protestant Reformation to their own favor – adopting the authoritarian Lutheran version as against the radical and libertarian expressions, which found more fertile ground in the Swiss cantons and the Dutch provinces, after the defeat of the great German peasant rising. The immediate effects of the Reformation in Scandinavia were, of course, the immense increase in crown lands and state revenues, while the religious changes were slower in the coming – commoners still worshipping the officially abandoned Catholic faith for decades to come. Thus, seen from the perspective of the ordinary peasant, the secular state machinery had merely engrossed its economic power base without sufficient justification – lest it may be consolidated through jurisdiction. The lack of internecine strife in Norway since the civil war era, which had come to an end in the early 13th century, rendered the state's military power less significant than for instance in England, where the Wars of the Roses in the 15th century nearly tore the country asunder – indeed, the conduct of all the Scandinavian peasants all the way into the Thirty Years' War, showed a deep suspicion towards the military adventures of their respective kings and commanders. Thus, while the militancy of the German peasants in the 1520's constituted one form of popular and regional transgression of the infant state's claim to a violence monopoly, the mass desertions and "peasant peaces"[4] in the border regions between the Scandinavian countries – which until recently had belonged to the common Kalmar Union, rendering all Scandinavians fellow citizens – was another variety of popular challenge against the consolidation of the modern state.

The anti-popular turn of the Reformation in Northern Europe after the German Peasants' War was launched with Luther's pamphlet, *Against the Robbing and Murdering Hordes of Peasants*. Lutheranism quickly turned into state ideology, and the irony of the pamphlet's title is glaring considering the fact that the German peasants were ruthlessly exploited by their lords, who also showed by far the greatest brutality during the armed struggle between them – as they were accustomed to do in times of peace – to the extent of having in the end to desist their slaughtering lest they would be bereft of a viable labor force. In such a context, it would seem highly necessary, for those who aimed at establishing and retaining power over peoples' souls, to redefine *the very concept of evil* itself, apparently in the form of "malevolent spirits conspiring with the Devil" – all the more since sporadic peasant rebellions broke out, especially in Northern Europe, throughout the rest of the century, and the heroic moments of 1524-25 lingered on in memory and passed from generation to generation in the form of strong folkloristic traditions. Indeed, as pointed out by some modern historians, "it is scarcely an exaggeration to say that the German peasants of 1525 anticipated most of the ideas of 1789".[5]

The German peasants' war capacity surpassed anything of its kind since the Spartacus revolt in ancient Rome, and its memory horrified rulers in the century to come, and more – as had the latter rising done sixteen centuries earlier – and the mere fact that it had struck right at the heart of the Holy Roman Empire itself added substantially to its psychological impact, and urgently induced secular powers to strive for control over the theoretical content of the Reformation. As for the German peasant armies, rather than consisting in a rabble of barely dressed and armed men, which one may have supposed from the time period in question and the peasants' social and economic position, quite to the contrary their troops were frequently equipped with considerable fire arms, cannons and cavalry – the resources of which they largely obtained from their urban allies; neither the industrious Hanseatic burghers had any love for idle nobles and a self-indulging clergy, or for toll imposing states, for that matter. There were troops of up to 10-12 000 peasant soldiers, waving red flags and fighting the injustices of the stagnant feudal system – a feudal system which was hardly more welcome among independence loving Norwegian and Swedish peasants when the numerous German fiefs were bequeathed land and taxation power in these regions through the dynastic maneuverings of the era. Even if the peasants of the vast German regions eventually were defeated, their militant risings had seriously disturbed the princely powers and upper classes, and the clampdown had been costly – in lives as well as financial resources. Thus, the presently ensuing *witch mania* constituted a highly welcome means against future disturbances – that is, outright rebellion against state authority – and by the time the religiously laden Thirty Years' War ended with the Peace of Westphalia in 1648, state machineries had been established to an unprecedented degree in modern Europe – in the coming to fruition of the precondition of the indispensible twin powers of any viable political entity; judicial hegemony and violence monopoly.

In the century preceding the ultimate consolidation of the modern states' military ascendancy it would seem fair to infer that the still reasonably feeble state machineries of Northern Europe had every reason to seek compensation through jurisdiction for whatever shortcomings there may have been with respect to their military control. This tendency, moreover, would seem to be increasingly important as "the power of the word" more than ever equaled "the power of the sword" – in a new era of printing presses and a higher premium on literacy, outside narrow clerical circles. The Reformation, in its manifold manifestations, was much more than a theological issue – however much the changes in the Christian faith has been emphasized by historians and taken as a matter of course by the general public; to borrow from the title of Perez Zagorin's work[6], for "rebel and ruler" in this tumultuous era it was first and foremost a question of political and economic power, and the battleground became increasingly an ideological one – potentially bereft of theological archaisms and nuances. It is easy, today, at a stage when state power largely is taken for granted, to underestimate its sense of precariousness and uneasiness in the years of its infancy; an infancy, moreover, which hardly could prove impervious to infantile resolutions – such as hazardous war campaigns and ideologically and religiously oriented persecution of "deviant" individuals.

The simple fact that the Reformation reoriented everyday focus towards *personal belief* constituted the very ideological and psychological preconditions for a phenomenon like the witch hunts to occur on a relatively mass scale. Fomented by heretical movements since the early Middle Ages this theological dictum surely represented a double edged sword for the reforming elites; the one edge of which being a decisive weapon against the vested powers of the Catholic clergy and its luxurious economic possessions; the other turning into a popular challenge against authority *as such* – which harmonized poorly with the ambitions of pretentious lay princes and the "god chosen" monarchs who aspired to autarchy in early modern times, as against the decentralized and largely confederated regions of Medieval Europe. To turn the "personal beliefs" among the common people (among whom 80-90 per cent were illiterate peasants until the Industrial Revolution, with a somewhat lower percentage in the early urbanized Low Countries and Northern Italy) against themselves, in the form of highlighting their dangers and criminalizing "deviations", such as was the case with the witch hunts, obviously turned out to be the ruling elites' favored means for dealing with this "back flip of the Reformation coin". No doubt, however infantile and cruel this program turned out to be – and it is hard to imagine how it could have proceeded otherwise – it proved to be highly successful as regards the narrow aim of consolidating state power, as much as it must be regretted both on behalf of the poor victims of the persecutions, and when viewed in the long term perspective of the two world wars in the 20th century and the disempowerment of the individual in the modern era. There is no mystery whatsoever in the fact that the infant early modern state turned to *divide and conquer* strategies – in times and places where there were little or no internecine strife; after all, the very earliest incentives towards territorial state power had its origins in regional conflicts among nobles as well as city burghers, spiced with peasant revolts – all of which justified its claim as an arbitrary and "neutral" power.[7] As an illustration of to what extent the court clearly saw the implications in the Machiavellian *divide and conquer* mechanisms is testified by a sober observation by a contemporary writer in England at the time when the witch hunts were about to take off, who concluded that "the solidarity of society would be endangered by a belief that made every man afraid of his neighbor".[8] Hence, what would seem as a grave concern for the benevolent humanist, may easily turn into a weapon for power seeking state authorities in quest for legitimacy. After all, any solidarity lost within a society must be compensated for by a superior authority – lest the lack of it plunges society into utter social fragmentation and chaos – and the witch hunts would fairly easily been quelled by the authorities (apart from the clergy) if they actually had had no stake in them. Thus, it appears hardly coincidental that one of the strongest proponents of both state power and the justifications of the witch hunts, the jurist Jean Bodin, lived and worked in France in the period preceding the rise to prominence of the most centralized of states in the era, in the reign of Louis XIV. Bodin, moreover, dedicated a lengthy discussion to the causes of revolutions throughout history, and was keenly concerned with the possible means at hand to avoid them, and regarding the significance of the witch hunts with respect to the modern state's quest for hegemony, the British witch monger, Joseph Glanvill, drew the following deduction in his zeal against "the wicked": "No witches, no, spirits, no immortality, no God."[9] One is surely tempted, in analyzing that era of "god given" monarchies, to add that without the witch mania there would hardly have been any consolidated European states either.

Judicial state measures

In Scandinavia, where there were faint popular protestant sentiments against the catholic clergy – and the papal power was relatively weak in any case – the infant states certainly utilized the authoritarian Lutheran creed for all it was worth, as illustrated by the fact that their courts and officials ingeniously and successfully applied the new dictum of *personal belief* as a means to sow and inflame suspicion and distrust among their subjects towards each other – especially by disrupting the very *oikos*, or household, sphere in attacking age old medicinal practices and herb utilization, and literally demonizing them under the general labels of "diabolic witchcraft" or, as in Denmark-Norway, *trolldomskunst*. It takes no great imaginative effort to recognize the highly effectual way in which such disruption of local communities, each of which meant "the World" for common people in the early modern era, would deflect the attention of peasants and urban poor from their crucial economic and political interests, and give leeway for a strengthening of the state apparatus. In fact, the "take off" of witch hunts in Norway, for example, coincides with Frederick II's frustrations with the notoriously disobedient peasant soldiers during the Nordic Seven Years' War (1563-70), even to the extent of massive fraternization between the peasants across the borders, and the monarch's consequent resolution to increase control over his northern province through the introduction of the two new administrative offices of *stattholder* and *sorenskriver*. The former was a general means to centralize authority in general, and especially tighten up military discipline, while the latter represented a sly way of subverting the peasants' time honored control over the basic law court – *bygdetinget*. Needless to say, this penetration into the basic judicial system and grass roots' social structure was necessary for the state authorities if they were to have any hope of successfully penalizing – through recurrent law edicts – and persecuting to the most horrendous degree, simple practices of herbalogy and "healing", conflating them with alleged "conspiracies with the Devil".

The main bulk of witches persecutions in Scandinavia occurred somewhat later than in Central Europe, a fact that fits well with the ordinary centre-periphery notion. Not only was the Reformation itself delayed, especially in Denmark-Norway (1536), but the scattered populations in topographic regions, only rarely in contact with the authorities, made the conversion an outdrawn process. Surely, a lawmaker or a law making body has to make their edicts properly known before it makes any sense to effectuate their demands and punish transgressions. Hence, there were very few executions in the first generation after the religious upheaval – in a period when the feeble state concentrated on expropriating the lands of the Catholic clergy to increase revenues needed for expanding the administrative apparatus. However, throughout this early Reformation era *recurrent local and regional peasant revolts* posed a need for the state to employ disciplining measures, most effectively achieved by deflecting the commoners focus from the engrossment of the state apparatus and its tax gatherers – in order to *divide and conquer*. In Denmark-Norway, at least, which is the region most closely studied by the present author, the number of peasant revolts and witch hunt processes are, indeed, conversely proportional throughout the early modern period, during which the state gained ascendancy over decentralized and confederal tendencies – and even invaded the conscience of the individual.

Thus in Denmark-Norway it is natural to date the initiation of systematic processes against the dissenting witches and *trollmenn* to the time period succeeding Frederick IIs jurisdiction of 1584/93 against *throldomskonst* (witchcraft). These new laws were enacted in the wake of exchanges with the Stavanger bishop, Jorgen Eriksson, who had reacted upon the proliferate "superstition" among the public in his region and the utilization by certain individuals of magical practices and appeal to "supernatural forces". This period was, as described in some detail elsewhere, marked by widespread peasant unrest and disobedience[12], and consequent reactionary and repressive measures taken by the monarch – as for example when he promoted the notorious peasant harasser, Ludvig Munk, to the position of *stattholder* in Norway after removing him from his fiefdom in Trondelag, where he had become immensely unpopular among the peasants.

The jurisdiction introduced by Frederick II was initially (1584) meant to apply only for the south-western Norwegian region around the city of Stavanger, but in 1593 it was expanded to encompass the whole country – most probably after the disciplining effects of the new laws in the Stavanger region were acknowledged by the king, while the insurgent peasantry was still threatening the control of the state officials elsewhere in the country and remained anti-militarist in orientation. That the Norwegian peasantry was far from affectionate towards the crown had proved all too clear to the king and his Danish court and generals during the Nordic Seven Years' War (1563-70); a war in which they had disobeyed his generals' command on a regular basis, consequently refused to charge into Swedish territories, and even held parties and fraternized with their Swedish "brothers" – before marching home to drumbeat and under flying banners, in a singularly proud form of desertion. In this context it would not seem far-fetched to expect, from an ambitious monarch probably intimately acquainted with Machiavellian statecraft, certain measures of *divide and conquer* tactics to strengthen the state apparatus and its control over popular mores and individual conduct. In fact, as already noted, the massive peasant unrest in Germany against their overlords in the 15th and early 16th century, culminating in the German Peasant War of the 1520's, corresponds fairly accurately with the beginning stages of the European witch hunts in exactly that part of the continent. While the conglomerate of small German states flourished economically in the High Middle Ages, propelled by the confederally organized Hanseatic League, their decline was monumental in the century culminating in the Thirty Years' War (1618-48). Hence, to retain power and resist confederal tendencies across state lines the princes had every reason to stir up mutual suspicion and fear among their subjects, and it comes as no surprise to learn that the fragmented German regions presented the most intensive witch persecutions throughout the whole actual period – easily transmitted to the countries in the North by the influx here of German fiefs and their ideology and experiences, an influx which was facilitated through dynastic ties between the North European courts, circulating *Malleus Malificarum* among themselves and the clergy.

For the centralized state to develop, mature and establish political hegemony over the various confederal structures and traditions throughout Europe, and eventually even wiping them out of public memory, in its initial stages it needs most of all to establish approximate military and judicial monopoly; for the subjects to play their part according to that monopoly satisfactorily they need to be disciplined, a discipline for which loyalty towards the crown is the most effective means – and this loyalty comes naturally with *fear* of – real or imagined – enemies within or without, and the subjects' consequent cry for protection; judge and general thus make the state consolidation process complete. With the development of standing armies, improved fire arms and cannons during the highly militarized 1600's, the states generally no longer needed fear insurrections from its own people, that is, before the "power of the word" exceeded the "power of the sword" in the Age of Democratic Revolutions which was fanned by a century of Enlightenment throughout Europe.

The degree to which the ideology of the ruling elites' and their political organization influenced on the extent of the witch mania, is highlighted by the most telling fact that in the tolerant and confederally structured Holland or, more properly, The United Dutch Provinces, only 150 persons were executed for witchcraft in early modern times, while in their neighbor country to the South, Belgium – largely affected by the dispositions of the centralizing French monarchy – 1600 persons were executed for the same reason in this era, the overall populations of the two countries being approximately the same. In this picture, it is worth noting that Catholic Spain – a long since established state at that stage in history – had very few processes and executions against alleged witches throughout the period, and imposed strict legal rules regarding the subject as early as 1614 – at an early stage in the Scientific Revolution. In Scotland, on the other hand, according to Christina Larner[13], ideological unification in combination with centralized state development was accompanied with, and facilitated through, the spiritually and morally "purifying" process of witch hunts. To illustrate the sense of uncertainty and anemia haunting the would-be autarchic rulers in early modern times, according to Palmer et. al.:

"As late as the 17th century, especially in Central Europe where the Thirty Years' War produced chaos and terror, kings and generals kept private astrologers to divine the future."[14]

The diversity of the persecuted beliefs and conducts

The wide variety of "crimes" which were persecuted under the general and convenient rubric *witchcraft*, as manifested in the law records from the period[15], seems at first bewildering and nonsensical. In the Nordic countries the terms *trolldom, diabolism, black magic* and even *white magic* were in use rather than the term *witchcraft*, which was only commonly used, in a somewhat humoristic manner, well into the Enlightenment era when the processes had faded into the history books. There seems to be but little resemblance between a *sami* shaman trying to influence living conditions through weather magic in Northern Scandinavia, and a woman with too outspoken sexual fantasies in some southern village community. Hence, to explain the witch hunt phenomenon simply as a matter of *patriarchy* is far from enlightening, even if it is an element of truth in it. One of the obvious reasons that *more* women than men were persecuted was, indeed, their challenge against the patriarchy of Church and state. With the Reformation the Catholic worship of Mary was eradicated by theological dogma, lending women's religious practices and personal behavior more readily to "demonological" scrutiny. However, when one takes a closer look, the various "offences" have one essential *transsexual* aspect in common: In their various ways they imply some form of *power* over daily life – or at least the very *belief* in such power – among the common people; an inherently sinister phenomenon for any ruler who might aspire to autarchy or absolutist rule. Thus, according to one of the ideologues *par excellence* as regarding early modern statecraft as well as witch hunting, Jean Bodin, "a sorcerer is one who by commerce with the Devil has a full attention of attaining his own ends"[16] At this stage in history, the ruler(s) being left in uncertainty, the looming question remains: Will "his people" nourish notions that they can do without a king and a central authority, for example in the way that they did in the prosperous United Dutch Provinces of that era?

As regards the state's "deflection tactics", the initial execution of witches in Norway, for example, occurred on the command of the fief, Erik Munk, in the 1570's, in the aftermath of the long and highly unpopular war between the Danish-Norwegian and Swedish crowns, and marked by intensive peasant risings against this fief for his harsh policies towards peasants and urban poor. It is of some importance to note that the year of the persecutions precedes the actual law edict on witchcraft (1584/93) with a decade or so, underpinning the underlying *realpolitik* dimensions of the persecutions and the consequent need for a judicial clampdown by the state. Moreover, the central period of witch hunts in Norway is 1620-1665, that is, during an intense period of warfare and the corresponding efforts by Christian IV and Frederick III to make loyal and obedient subjects out of a peasantry which for numerous generations had been inclined towards war resistance and fraternization across the Swedish border. Hardly coincidentally a professional standing army was established by 1660-70, in the same period as the witch hunts began to ebb out. Hence neither did legislation *launch* the witch hunts, in some kind of "moral crusade", nor did it *abolish* them "in the name of humanism and pity" – they were largely a question of simple power politics and tactics; for the crown, *stattholder* and ruling elite, in short, how to make loyal subjects, obedient tax payers, and efficient soldiers.

At the early stages of the witch hunts in Denmark-Norway the authorities cracked down on the two forms of magic practiced by the dissenting witches – males as well as females – more precisely black magic (*maleficium*), white magic and so-called "wise women". However, it was only with Christian IVs judicial reforms of 1617 that the processes against witchcraft took off, and there were even certain chain processes in which the accused and convicted witches, often after being tortured, revealed other people whom they claimed to be involved in the same practices or "conspiracy". With the judicial reforms of 1617 even diabolism (a "compact with the Devil") was encompassed by the legal code against witchcraft, and it is this latter variety which in certain instances led to such chain processes all over Europe, including the Nordic countries. It was, however, the two first mentioned categories which dominated in the witch hunts of the North, which in Norway alone led to ca. 730 executions according to modern data. From 1584 onwards in Denmark-Norway the punitive reaction was marked by the mosaic principle that went like "don't let a witch live" – that is, death sentence, either by burning or beheading – in *both* instances of magic. However, from 1617 onwards and the new legal code introduced in that year, the authorities took a softer attitude towards the various forms of white magic, resulting in punishments consisting in exile and confiscation of property for those "offences" – which indeed was a severe enough penalty, say, for growing and using herbs or praying to some "Sea spirit" for fair sailing weather. This new orientation towards white magic probably originated in the acknowledgement by the authorities in Copenhagen that it was somewhat "out of proportions" to penalize with death a basic part of the popular culture and the age old medicinal practices represented by so-called "white magicians". On the other hand, any form of diabolism or black magic was to be punished with death, so the question remained how to keep up the very *belief* in such faculties – in an age when modern science and urge towards rational explanations began to proliferate, especially along the coastlines of Europe.

I Norway it is the major cities along the coastline, especially Stavanger and Bergen, and also the Northern county of Finmark, which were home to the highest number of legal process against accused witches. The explanation for this phenomenon has generally been that the harsh climatic conditions in the coastal areas and their strong dependence on ocean travel (within fisheries and trade) during time immemorial had given rise to the practice of weather magic in the form of attempts at making favorable conditions for sea farers when it was a question of white magic; alternatively bad weather when the magical formula and practices originated in black magic. The processes in Finmark testify to aspects of demonology which was developed in early modern times in combination with the appeal to supernatural powers, such as in the rest of the country, but only in addition to aspects from the shamanist practices of the aboriginal Sami people – in other words, their tribal religion. However, witch hunts occurred all over the country, even if there were huge regional and local variations. Thus, there could be a huge amount of processes in one fiefdom or county, while they were almost absent in the neighboring one. Two main factors should be considered in this respect: The militarily strategic location of the actual fiefdom, and the personal character and degree of Enlightenment in the respective fief or judge (*sorenskriver*) – the latter variable becoming increasingly important towards the finishing stages of the processes in Europe generally.

Among the central scientific issues relating to the witch hunts has been whether they arose from disputes, slander and charges between people in the local communities and neighborhoods, or whether they were initiated through judicial ordinances by the government and the theology of the clergy, as expressions of the demonology of this pre-enlightened era. My own perspective tries to avoid this rigid dichotomy, because of an effort to see the "bigger picture" and disclose the complexities of the era. There is every reason to believe that the ideological aspect – the demonology dating back to the publication of the Witch Hammer in the late 15th century – must be seen as the decisive factor regarding *the content of the belief in witchcraft*. However, ideology is rarely more than a *power tool*, and the ideology of demonology proved singularly efficient regarding the monarchical facilitation of the immense increase in state power throughout the 16thand 17th centuries, and the corresponding conformity and obedience at the secular (military, taxation, etc.) as well as the religious level. Strained relationships between the members of local communities (arising from economic inequality and envy), and social stress factors such as ill harvest, dearth and starvation, had occurred for quite some time before the witch hunts were initiated. At the same time these latter social tensions – which accelerated in this period marked by population growth and resource pressures – were undoubtedly co-factors which could propel the processes, especially after 1584 when they could be reinforced by a demonologically oriented state power which posited the judicial means to clamp down on witchcraft on a broad scale. To the extent that local slander among the commoners instigated witch persecutions, which certainly could occur when the "campaign" was launched by the authorities, the very fact that about 50 % of those charged with accusations of witchcraft were acquitted only underpinned the power of the state apparatus and its legal courts. Had nearly all of them been convicted, it would have given the impression that the "word of the public" weighed quite as heavy as the "word of the state". This overwhelming elitist perspective will also be employed in the subsequent discussion of the ending of the witch hunts around 1700, especially since there is but little which testify to lessening stress factors between the common people towards the end of the 17th century compared to the previous period, as long as Europe in general was marked by economic stagnation in this period and well into the 18th century. Hence, we must again turn to political power aspects and ideological questions to clarify the abandonment of the witch persecutions – which, however, were "reincarnated" in persecutions of Jews, gypsies, homosexuals, and other marginalized people, in subsequent centuries – especially in times of great turmoil and distress.

Early modern skepticism and Renaissance Humanism

It is often conveniently assumed that the witch hunts were a predominantly religious phenomenon, and that the main persecutors were the clergy. The reader will have noticed that this position is challenged by the present author who, however, has no intention to dismiss the role of religion altogether – least of all regarding the Reformation processes and its repercussions; but then again the Reformation – as a societal phenomenon – was largely a question of *political and economic power.* Anyway there were numerous orthodox Protestants, as for example the British theologian, John Webster[17], who stressed the perverting of Christians' imagination by the incessant exposure to the vilest accusations and the most obscene "confessions" – the latter regularly delivered under torture, the restrictions of which immediately caused the number of positive sentences to decline. As there were doubting theologians there were necessarily skeptics among the judges who, however, feared reprisals from the crown, the rage of the people, and charge of atheism in the mix of issues at stake in this problem complex which converge around the very core of the power issue as such. The early skeptics most certainly were inspired by their own conscience and common sense, as well as by the spread of scientific discoveries which were made from the 16th century onwards – gradually staking out a largely *secular* direction among the nations of Europe. Furthermore, the writings of such leading humanists as Hugo Grotius (1583-1645), who stressed essentially *rational* judicial principles, and Michel de Montaigne (1533-1592), who initiated the modern *skeptical* tradition with his standard question, *What do I know?*, as well as Francois Rabelais' (1490-1553) thought provoking use of *irony* against high and low in his writings, eventually made it increasingly difficult to refer to Spränger, Kramer and Bodin's work when dealing with the conscience of the individual as well as the procedures of law. Hence, as the belief in supernatural powers declined, the phenomena pertaining to the witch hunts were increasingly analyzed in the light of psychological disturbances and sociopathic eruptions – in short, it became increasingly untenable even to *believe in* the magical power of witchcraft, before it ultimately ended up in the categories of illusion and humor – that is, when the states were firmly established. In England, a final and definitive blow to the very belief in occult powers in the early Enlightenment era occurred with Francis Hutchinson's summary, *Historical Essay on Witchcraft* (1718), and in Denmark-Norway in the first half of the 18th century, Enlightenment philosopher, Ludvig Holberg, wrote humoristic epistles about the bygone witch mania.

The historically rapid abandonment of the witch hunts towards the end of the 17th century has been among the subjects which have puzzled researchers into the phenomenon. In our context it is necessary to point out that little as these processes originated in the Nordic countries, just as little did their waning begin in this peripheral European region. Central Europe – especially the German states – was a forerunner in initiating the witch hunts as well as lagging behind when it came to abandoning them. However, the Nordic countries followed closely the German developments, as an integrated part of the Western cultural sphere and through the ties between the Germanic part of the continent and the Oldenburghian Danish court, German fiefs both in Sweden and Norway, and so on. Thus, there is no doubt that we are dealing with common European social processes and ideological currents, even if they manifested themselves through diverging national and regional expressions, and some corners were more strongly pledged to religious tolerance and confederalism – or simply were early consolidated Catholic states largely impervious to the very notion of witchcraft. Europe in the 16th to 18th century was far less dominated by enclosed national patterns than later on in the modern era, as testified by the immense proliferation and influence of *The Republic of Letters* which circulated Enlightenment sentiments in the heyday of secularism and faith in progress during the 18th century – in the spirit of the confederal organization patterns which contested with state power well into the early modern era.

In Europe the intensity of the witch hunts was significantly reduced while The Thirty Years' War

(1618-1648) raged at its worst in the respective countries, during which the fronts initially were delineated between catholic and protestant states. During the Danish-Norwegian entanglement in this protracted war, in 1625, the same thing happened in these countries, especially in Eastern Norway and the Danish part of the dual monarchy.[18] Thus, the question naturally arises whether the general image of the external foes during this conflict resulted in lessened stress on the internal ones – represented by the witches and dissenters in general. Throughout history a common historical trait in various stages of political centralization and consolidation of state power has been a seemingly recurring need among those in power to single out foes who are charged of threatening the unity and security of the respective states, if only to achieve loyalty and obedience among its subjects. This ideological device was especially utilized during the age of aspiring absolutism, in which all power was held to derive directly from god. The fact that the witch hunts declined so considerably in intensity during intensive battle periods of The Thirty Years War indicates that the authorities at this stage had more than enough in dealing with their foreign enemies, and more or less ignored their internal ones – whether because of lacking resources or lack of need and motivation to single out internal enemies of the state during the international strife. The fact is, however, that the witch hunts were intensely reinforced immediately after the Peace of

Westphalia was signed in 1648, and raged on for another half century before their abrupt cessation towards the end of the century.

About the mid 17th century more and more theologians all over Europe started to lose interest in witchcraft. The clergy had played a prominent role in the elaboration of demonology in collaboration with jurists and scholars in statecraft, such as Bodin (1530-96), as well as participating in the legal processes against the accused witches. Even if the judicial processes after the Reformation was transferred to the secular authorities and the king himself became head of the church, it is highly probable that a diminishing interest among the clergy in the struggle against witchcraft influenced on the attitude among the secular authorities towards the phenomenon as well. After the conclusion of The Thirty Years' War, Lutheran Protestantism consolidated its position in Central and Northern Europe, concomitantly with diminishing expressions of Judgment Day and Millenarian notions which had been circulating in Europe continent ever since the heretical movements of the early Middle Ages, surging once again with the outbreak of The Black Death in the late 1340s, and reinforced immediately after the Reformation was launched in 1517. The wars of religion in the post-Reformation era, and the theological, ideological and socio-economic insecurity resulting from the great Reformation turmoil, contributed to what some researchers have designated as traits of "mass psychosis" in early modern Europe. This immense unrest and uncertainty culminated in The Thirty Years War, and after its conclusion the new Protestantism entered its consolidated stage. Thus, when the papacy in 1676 declared that "In Rome we don't believe in witchcraft", the protestant clergy would rather not be less "enlightened", in an age when new scientific discoveries by figures like Galilei (1564-1642) and a new, rational way of thinking among philosophers like René Descartes (1596-1650) and G. W. Leibniz (1646-1716) was presented to the literate segments of the public. All of these central figures in the history of European ideas conferred a central position to god in their writings and world view, and were to represent a huge challenge for the orthodox theologians during the time period when the witch hunts were abandoned. Thus, science, theology and philosophy became parts of a nexus of impacts which in time came to push European societies into an enlightening, rationalist and progressive direction, and the belief in witchcraft among the social elites was increasingly regarded as a fallacy belonging to the past. According to historian, Solvi Sogner: "With the modern breakthrough, the witch hunt processes were ultimately to be considered as inconsistent with the spirit of progress"[19], echoing Francis Bacon's and Descartes' early modern equation: Knowledge and power makes for progress.

Decisive developments towards ending the witch hunts

The very consolidation stage of the early modern state's political hegemony coincides with three crucial developments: The culmination of the Scientific Revolution, the development of unprecedented armaments, and the new economic doctrines of *mercantilism* – all of which beginning in the economically most pulsating regions of Europe and spreading gradually to the more peripheral corners. Before the Scientific Revolution the obsession with witchery had been challenged by some theologians on the religiously based foundations that contracts between the Devil and those whom he already controlled, were absurd; that the Devil would never let himself be controlled by some miserable woman (or man); and that god's providence would never allow "his children" to be let so far astray. However, the commonsensical reasonableness of these still fairly orthodox arguments weren't enough against the ideologically accumulated mass hysteria, fuelled by state persecutions in the period when the infant state were in dire need to demonstrate its power towards, and establish discipline among, those whom it claimed to be its subjects. With the new scientific orientation, however, enlightened ideas reinforced former objections, in time causing the state to recognize far better ways of spending human resources than outdrawn law suits dealing with largely noncommunicable phenomena, and haphazardly resulting either in incomprehensible acquittal or the wanton consummation of human flesh in the allegedly "purifying" flames. In the Nordic countries, as standing professional armies finally were raised in the wake of the Thirty Years' War the troublesome and confederally oriented war resistance and "peasants' peaces" were done with, and the crown had laid the basic foundation for establishing an elaborate state apparatus.

It is hardly accidental that the most prosperous and tolerant country throughout the 17th century, Holland, or more precisely The United Dutch Provinces, was the home of the scrupulously systematical and influential philosopher, Baruch Spinoza (1632-77); his pantheistic and tolerant philosophy implied that "god" exists in everything and everyone. According to Palmer, et. al., the Dutch republic in the 17th century "enjoyed a degree of comfort and of intellectual, artistic, and commercial achievement unexcelled in Europe".[20] Significantly, religious toleration was introduced in the United Dutch Provinces already in 1632, and their republican officials became highly influential in international diplomacy, as they toned down militarism to the least possible degree – even to the extent of largely keeping this north western European region out of the Thirty Years War. Admittedly, the introduction of religious tolerance in the United Dutch Provinces was largely motivated by the fear of alienating the Catholics in the area and their possible alignment with Catholic Spain, which remained a continuous threat against the Dutch in the late 16th and early 17th century. However, the economic and cultural effects of this high premium on toleration proved to be illustratively fruitful – and, in time, an example to be admired and implemented by increasingly secularized states throughout Europe, for example exemplified in the British Toleration Act of 1688.

Spinoza's ethical work appeared in 1670 and espoused the idea that the Bible was a work for moral guidance rather than a "fountain of truth" in an encompassing sense – a case which had come to the fore after the scientific discoveries during his lifetime had muted the wildest claims concerning nature and reality in the biblical scriptures. Significantly, he was appointed to a university lecturing position in Heidelberg in 1673, and from what we know about his immense influence in learned circles at the time – and the intimate contact between the German states and the Scandinavian countries – it would not be far-fetched to indicate that his philosophy and teaching had its share in the judges gradually turning their deaf ear on tales of "evil spirits" and "compacts with the Devil". Certainly, he exercised some influence across the channel too, and later in the 1670's a theologian, John Webster, who had long been opposed to the belief in witchcraft, published his *The Displaying of Supposed Witchcraft*, in which he summarized the objections of previous decades – as for example the role played by imagination. In 1691, another Dutchman, Balthassar Bekker, published his *World Bewitched*, with the intention to strike a final blow against the belief in witchcraft. It appeared, however, at a time when only a very few judges could be found who were prepared to convict people for "crimes" which learned men generally pitied or laughed at. The witch craft panic lasted longest in Germany and Central and Eastern Europe, where state consolidation still was going on, a fact that underpins the *divide and conquer* perspective. Another fact, that the very final execution for witchcraft took place in Scotland in 1722 – in a period when Scottish independence currents ran high – also point towards this basic explanation of the form and extent of the phenomenon.

In England, where the new scientific ideas got a stronghold at a very early stage, with contributions from central figures such as Francis Bacon (1561-1626) and Isaac Newton (1642-1727), crucial developments took place toward ending the witch hunts, in the decades before the adoption of its Toleration Act concerning religious matters – a turn of events undoubtedly to a considerable extent imported from "tolerant Holland". Thus, in the 1660's there were references to a new generation of enlightened judges who gave small or no encouragement to accusations of witchcraft. Ideas moved relatively fast in early modern Europe, especially in coastal areas, and the above mentioned tendency among judges seems to have become more and more common in major parts of its North- and Northwestern countries in the second half of the 17th century. No doubt the Renaissance in Northern Europe – most notably in the Low Countries – with its emphasis on humanism, human rights and equitable jurisdiction, also had its long term impact on the administrators of the law, alongside the more recent scientific requirements as regards proofs. The institutionalization of science in England, in the form of the Royal Scientific Society of London, founded 1662, to be followed up by a Royal Academy of Sciences in France in 1666, implied a new intellectual atmosphere in which a wide specter of new knowledge, from the natural sciences to legal history, were combined – even in the single researcher. As regards the growing philosophy of "Natural law", Palmer, Colton and Kramer states that:

"This philosophy, developed by the Greeks and renewed in the Middle Ages, held that the Universe is fundamentally orderly and that there is a natural rightness or justice, *universally the same for all people* and *knowable by reason.*"[21]

Thus, for any intellectually oriented and well informed person in the early modern era – especially when the various states had largely consolidated its judicial and military power – it would have been easy, for example contemplating Newton's law of gravity, to ridicule and laugh at the very notion of a witch riding through thin air on a wooden stick, on her way to a "date with the Devil", or a Nordic shaman throwing pigs in the ocean to incur favorable wind. In short, the subscription to superstitious beliefs became increasing untenable for any learned person. Moreover, the fact that most of the early modern scientifically oriented minds, from Descartes to Newton, kept their own faith in religion (in the form of what came to be known as *deism*, which reduced the role of god to a prime mover, or "watchmaker"), posed a new challenge to theological orthodoxy far more momentous than some shaman worship here and diabolism there. The very recognition that humanity was no longer the centre of the Universe, had the immediate result of producing a temporary humility in human affairs – a form of *catharsis* which evolved into a new self-confidence within the ruling elite, as scientists increasingly replaced theologically inclined individuals in the state administrations, which could no longer bow to flagrant superstition. The new requirement of evidence, at the expense of faith and revelation, meant that a judge who aimed at mastering the "state of the art" within his discipline concluded that law sentence without evidence equaled primitiveness, and after 1650 mere hearsay was dismissed by the new generation of scientifically oriented judges, while it had been more than enough to send people to the "purifying flames" a generation earlier. Confessions obtained under torture was accordingly disqualified as evidence, as the new embryonic humanist sciences produced a better understanding of what human beings might do or say to escape unbearable pain. Voluntary confessions, which were rarer, were referred to the mundane diagnosis of hysteria and psychosis. Thus, humanism, medicine and professionalized law courts combined neatly to conclude a singularly embarrassing chapter in early modern history. When the state's power had been consolidated – judicially and militarily – it need no longer fear large united masses of people in revolt, even fighting for confederal ties with the subjects of a dynastic rival. Thus, the judicial elite shifted focus from the witch mania to more fruitful subjects – such as property rights, tolls and taxation.

In the aftermath of the Scientific Revolution, as Notestein put it, "the combatants [in the witch dispute] were now to fight over the reality and unreality of supernatural phenomena"[22], considerably reducing the role of the clergy and its orthodox theology; hence the fairly self-evident fact that the clergy alone could never have been able to make such a magnified cause of the belief in witchcraft without the aid of a state apparatus – the two of them being mutually dependant of each other, most of all in times of social unrest and tendencies towards revolts and insurgencies. Hence, when the state officials lost interest in the witch issue in favor of the new scientific rationalism – realizing the hugely beneficial economic utility of the latter – witch hunting was a lost cause. Naturally, the commoners in general – even if largely illiterate – easily turned against absurd superstition as such, when the fear of being victimized for "trivial pursuits" or mental disorders was appeased, and new rationalistic ideas were propounded by the authorities in the public sphere, most notably by judges and attorneys who certainly belonged to the most enlightened people in the latter half of the 17th century.

As much as the weakness of the state was closely connected with the start of the witch hunts, which occurred in border regions with persisting confederal traditions and institutions, the end developments of these persecutions – which had their last repercussions in areas marked by slow communications and spread of ideas (especially in the inner regions of Central and Eastern Europe) where secessionist movements may even have threatened – are significantly overlapping with the increasing consolidation of its power. In the aftermath of the Scientific Revolution the old monarchical notion of the king as "god's representative on Earth" became increasingly untenable – as the claim of biblical truth was shattered by the discovery and explanation of natural laws. Moreover, the huge secularization of European society resulting from this metaphysical loop, far surpassing that of the Reformation era, involved an unprecedented orientation towards *economics* – in the form of *mercantilism*. The state apparatus was professionalized and, at the very apex, new state departments of trade, finances, taxation and revenue drew considerable, and sometimes even overwhelming, attention to socio-economic aspects of government and the productivity of its subjects. Hence, the demand for "personal belief" initially inherent in Reformation ideologies, but subsequently submitted to state orthodoxy, was effectively deflected by the state into the "riches of personal productivity", achieved by the individual who succeeded in the de-sublimation of his or her spiritual powers (as a *Homo Faber*) into brute labor force (*animal laborans*). Thus, the spiritual and cultural aspects of life were toned down, disciplined standing armies had been produced in the wake of the Thirty Years War – and by the end of the 17th century armed mass insurgencies against the state seemed quite inconceivable, even as the tremendous socio-economic changes produced *unprecedented divisions* within early modern society which required the closest attention from the head of state and his ministers.

The effects of the mercantilist state ideology, focusing on the economically productive aspects of social life, were truly formidable; the focus on mines and metals induced a need for hugely increased labor force, the professional standing army needed salaries, as did the civil officials, and any notion of wasting the commoner's energy on wasteful issues seemed glaringly counterproductive. Thus, any schooled burgher or civil servant in the mid 17th century may easily have ridiculed the witch tales from "murky corners" – and may even have been abhorred by the use of torture and the bestial executions. In an age which increasingly oriented itself according to the *idea of progress*, cruel executions for irrationally founded "quasi-crimes" have a singularly disharmonious ring to it. It is certainly also highly probable that the peasants and poor town folk, as they eventually started to achieve some property rights, and became independent artisans or yeomen, soon became far too busy running their new or reinvigorated businesses to indulge in speculation about the spiritual life of a somewhat "idiosyncratic" woman or man in the neighborhood. It goes without saying that frustrated people, or people under certain stress, more readily end up chasing scapegoats for their own malaise – either in the form of each other or the authorities or, under special circumstances, foreign people – than industrious ones who glances prosperity on the horizon.

As we have seen, it was in Western Europe that the new rationalist ideas originated and became most widespread from the second half of the 17th century onwards, a fact that to a certain degree explains why the witch hunts proceeded unremittingly in Eastern parts of Europe well into the 18th century – in areas where Enlightenment sentiments were much slower to develop and proliferate. As regards the Nordic countries, which according to their geographical location always have belonged to the periphery when it comes to the introduction of new, guiding cultural impulses, we certainly have to consider additional regional factors to elucidate the end developments of the witch hunts in this region. In this respect, it is relevant to draw attention to the introduction of absolutism in the Danish state, including the duchies Schleswig and Holstein and Norway, in 1660, and the immensely more efficient central and local administration resulting from this change, especially regarding the supervision of official servants within the judicial apparatus and the standardization of their tenure within the legal system at large. The transition to absolutism largely eliminated the opportunities for individual civil servants to follow their own ill-founded inclinations and prejudices even when it came to witch hunt processes.

To go into some more detail regarding the abandonment of the witch hunts towards the end of the 17th century, it is relevant to draw attention to the activities of cantonal judge Mandrup Schönneböl in the county of Finmark from the 1650s onwards. After several actions taken by the judge, by which he manages to stop the persecutions temporarily and release the accused, he manages to put a definitive end to the processes in 1663, and during the 1660s the same reforming atmosphere reaches the counties of Trondelag and counties even further south. This happened despite the fact that accusations continued to well up from the grassroots of society and the various local communities and neighborhoods in the respective regions, among people who had been accustomed to the demonization of claimed "supernatural powers". During the 17th century the cantonal judges became immensely better schooled judicially than in former periods, and their improvement put them in a position to evaluate and rectify the procedures at the lower judicial levels in the local communities, which had conducted the sentences in cases of witchcraft. The investigations by the cantonal judges revealed for example apparent violations of the statutes of 1547/48 (a generation before the jurisdiction on witchcraft was introduced) which stated clearly that torture may not be used during interrogations of persons accused of various crimes, and that revelations by the accused of other persons as witches were not to be heeded. For the most part this latter guideline had been followed in Denmark-Norway, as testified by the fact that chain processes were the exception here, the exception being the county of Finmark. Through the cantonal judges' intervention in these cases the use of torture in legal processes was abolished, including the infamous water test, and so was the proliferation of false accusations; accordingly it became safer for close relatives of the accused to testify to their innocence. During the most intensive stage of the witch hunts testifying in favor of the accused, which practically was the only way to absolve them of the charges, had been a very risky venture – because by doing so the testifier was apt to be judged on a par with the accused and become a victim of the same process.

There is little reason to believe that these new judicial measures on behalf of the cantonal judges originated in their own individual minds and that they acted solely on their own initiative. On the contrary, they must be viewed in the context of the new rationalist ideas which were proliferating to an increasing extent among the European social elites in the latter half of the 17th century. Underlying the ideological changes which by the 1670's and 80's caused the administrators of the law to disbelieve accusations of witchcraft – and even acknowledge the validity of certain insights within the so-called white magic practices of herbalogy – was the recognition of the vastly increased state power at that stage compared with the initial stages of witch hunting. As the state's need for demonstrations of force in the form of persecuting stigmatized people faded with the declining intensity of peasant rebellions, the new mercantilist orientation among the ruling elites soon got a strong foothold within the state administration; tax rebellions were almost unheard of by the end of the 17t century, and war resistance a thing of the past, too. The development of the administrative apparatus – at the central as well as the local level – necessarily resulted in a new professionalism within the judicial system, including stricter demands on the presentation of "evidence" against people accused of witchcraft. Indeed, during a transitional period several local judges, bailiffs and clergymen were sentenced to pay high fees for inappropriate and illegal proceedings against the accused, including the use of torture, with the consequent reparations to be paid to the victims. Concomitantly with this development there was submitted an increasing number of appeals to higher judicial levels all the way to the Supreme Court, and there was a tendency that these higher – and more professional – judicial agents produced milder sentences than those at the local judicial level. This fact also underpins the so-called "top-down" perspective as part of an explanatory model for the abandonment of the witch hunt processes in Denmark-Norway around 1670. With respect to this date it is worth noting that it was immediately before the outbreak of a new war between Denmark-Norway and Sweden; the so-called "Feud of Gyldenlöve" which lasted from 1675-79 and involved one of the first serious tests for the new professionalized army. Surely, no disruptive internal law suits regarding increasingly untenable accusations were considered welcome by the state authorities in this period.

A disputed issue has been whether Christian V's Norwegian law of 1687 may have contributed to the end of the witch hunts. There is little to underpin such a suggestion. Firstly, the law does not state anything new regarding witchcraft; quite to the contrary, the ordinances from 1617 are maintained and they are even kept all the way to 1842. Secondly, these processes had practically ceased before the decree of the new legal code of 1687, which replaced Magnus Lagaböte's "Law of the Land" in 1274 – with some minor modifications in Christian IV's Norwegian law of 1604. Thus, we are confronted with an illustrating development in which the new and more modern ideas and attitudes among leading representatives of the state administration – mostly of Danish and German origin – were not materialized in the law code. In an age of absolutism, however, this fact is not peculiar at all. This was a period in which the legal code was, to a large extent, the personal work of the king himself – deriving his power "directly from god" – and it is a well known case that several of the absolutist monarchs throughout history did not belong to the most updated and enlightened characters in their own time. The Danish-Norwegian kings towards the end of the 17th century – Frederick IV and Christian V – were strongly influenced by the courts in other parts of Europe, which resisted political and legal reforms all the way until the Age of Democratic Revolution in the latter half of the 18th century. Hence, the quest for *power* motivated *jurisdiction*, and not the other way around. The fact that the law code of 1617 was maintained in the new laws of 1687 may probably also be ascribed to a general *judicial conservatism* which had existed in the Nordic countries ever since the Viking Age – a trend that is illustrated by the fact that the "Law of the Land" in Norway from 1274, which for its own part represented a continuation of the old regional law codes dating all the way back to the 9th century, was maintained into the modern era.

In Europe at large nearly 50 percent of the witch trials in the early modern period ended with acquittal for those who were subjects to persecution, and the percentage was relatively high even at the early and the most intensive stages of the phenomenon. This fact has induced some historians to conclude that the witch hunts were *initiated from below*, as a result of social stresses in the form of hunger, diseases, etc. throughout Europe in the actual time period. However, even if a certain need to find scapegoats when things go wrong will always be a factor to consider in relation to mass persecutions, it remains a fact that the ideological basis (*demonology*) for state involvement in for example the eventual rights and wrongs of age old medicinal practices, *preceded* the witch mania itself – fuelled by priests from the pulpit and judges in the court. Hence, rather than weakening the *divide and conquer* perspective put forth in this essay, I would contend that the fact of relatively numerous acquittals quite to the contrary strengthened the state all the more; people remained divided and in uncertainty, both accused and accuser increasingly lost their remaining confidence in their own power, while the state consolidated the essential building block of its own – jurisdictional strength and legitimacy, without which cannon and gunfire is largely useless when it comes to the formation of obedient and productive subjects.

Throughout the 16th and 17th centuries the state's direct power over the individual – his or her soul no less than their physical life – largely outmatched the political alternatives to the centralized state, notably confederated regions and cities. Thus throughout the witch hunt period the Hanseatic League faded into history, the Swiss confederacy lost its prominence and vitality, and even the United Dutch Provinces tended in an increasingly centralizing direction, while the absolutist monarchies of France as well as Denmark-Norway consolidated their position, and monarchical power was strengthened even in "parliamentarian" England and aristocratic Prussia. There can hardly be any doubt that the socially disrupting witch hunts, and the state's judicial role in them, were indispensable for this relatively rapid consolidation of state institutions which otherwise would seem to be unnecessary, and even abhorrent, to the commoner – especially in regions with strong confederal traditions. Thus, when the state's legitimacy was established through jurisdiction, it had laid the foundation for military discipline among peasant soldiers, who formerly had proved largely unwilling and in part been in possession of judicial power at that; and at that stage in this consolidation process when ideological, jurisdictional and military power was elevating the states far above the heads of individuals and their respective regions, the very *raison d'etre* for the witch hunts, seen from the power oriented and increasingly enlightened statesman's point of view, speedily evaporates.

As regards the grassroots perspective, such as presented internationally by historians like the British Macfarlane and in Scandinavia by Hans Eyvind Naess, pressures from the public – as *a result of* social strain factors like dearth and hunger – has been relegated to a secondary role in this essay. The justification for the emphasis on the *top-down-perspective*, apart from the obvious *divide and conquer* motivations, is that social strife and stress factors hardly were a novel phenomenon towards the end of the 16th century, at the time when the witch hunts took off; thus, they cannot constitute sufficient reasons for the initiation of the processes we are discussing. Correspondingly, they can neither be regarded as satisfactory explanations of the abandonment of the witch hunts, by referring to a lessening of the social stress factors – which did not ebb before way into the 18th century, long after the witch hunts had lost the attention of the crown's judicial representatives. It has been noted that the accusations continued to flow into the hands of the authorities in Denmark-Norway even after 1670, but at this stage they fell dead and powerless to the ground because of the new enlightened spirit within the judicial apparatus, if not within the narrow circles of the Danish court, which anyhow had reached a new level of confidence in its own powers and in the loyalty of its subjects. The ideology among the social elites had changed drastically since the heyday of demonology; theologians had largely lost interest in the issues of witchcraft, and a rationalist and mercantilist focus had got a hold on the outlook and dispositions of the state officials. However, it remains a reasonably astonishing fact that since the legal ordinance of 1617 remained in force as regards witchcraft in Christian V's law of 1687, judges were still *formally* ordered to persecute witches of any kid and strike down hard at their magical practices; hence, the negligence of the legal code by these officials after ca. 1670 must be seen as a form of "civil disobedience" towards the king himself and his judicial intentions. One relevant aspect of the endurance of the jurisdiction on witchcraft is, of course, the universal inertia of legal systems in relation to the incessant flow of thoughts and economic change; hence, the most reasonable explanation for the leniency shown by the king towards his "disobedient" civil servants is that the strong currents of new Enlightenment ideals surging all over Europe – stressing *progress* and *civic virtue* – at an early stage proved to be an irresistible force which laid the ideological foundation for the Age of the Democratic Revolution in the latter half of the 18th century, and ultimately paved the way for the fall of absolutism in France and elsewhere. The new credo of the Enlightenment era, the initiation of which concurred with the consolidation of the modern states and the end of the witch hunts, stressed the need for enlightened *virtue* among civilized peoples – propounded by writers such as Dryden, Bayle, Locke and Shaftesbury towards the end of the 17th century – directing attention towards rational matters and inveighing against tendencies fostering fraction. However, the consolidation of the modern European states had its stunningly costly price, not only in the very torture and pain inflicted on devious and idiosyncratic individuals labeled as witches in the early modern period; the very centralization of power itself was to haunt civilization into our own time, as the various states – in various degrees – succumbed to jingoist and militarist agendas, even recycling the essentials of the witch hunts in the form of persecuting Jews and gypsies, among others.

Conclusion

Among the many convergences of significant phenomena and developments in the early modern era, the witch hunts occurred during the early growth of the *bourgeoisie*, which in its early stages had strong ties to the rural population. Together ambitious burghers and angry peasants constituted a tremendous socio-economic force – as testified during the German Peasants War in the early 1500's – represented by collective entities which even to a large extent attended to their matters in a confederal manner, and hence constituted major obstacles to the consolidation of the state in most parts of Europe. The *feudal* state was based on the clergy and the nobility, both of which tended in a decentralizing direction through their bishoprics and fiefdoms. Then, after commerce had taken off in the wake of the Portuguese and Spanish "discoveries" in the Americas, including the greatest robbery of precious metals ever, followed by the virulent trading activity of Antwerp, including the inception of modern banking, by the first half of the 16th century, cities in coastal parts of Europe were swelled with burghers drawn there by the new vocational opportunities – or forced off their lands by warfare, if they had not merely been superfluous in agrarian activity because of increasing productivity *per capita* as a result of new agricultural techniques and methods. A considerable number of people also simply fled from their landlords and threw off the yoke of serfdom. In this turbulent period burghers grew increasingly prosperous and self-centered, while gradually losing their rural roots and mores, and in time enabled the stagnant states to substitute its defunct ideological (clerical) and economical (feudal) basis with a new and more promising one. The *bourgeois* privileges granted by the royal courts (with the notable exception of France), for example the British Navigation Act of 1651 and various edicts favoring the *bourgeoisie* in Denmark/Norway in 1660-90, summarizes this story very briefly and concisely. During these developments altogether new constellations between the various estates and classes in society unfolded – and these abruptly introduced complexities were far from stable and harmonious; new internal antagonisms came to the fore – town versus country, artisans versus bourgeoisie, etc – rendering state propelled witch hunts utterly obsolete and useless seen from a power oriented statesman's point of view.

Thus, with the new social forces of internecine disruptions – real and threatening ones, rather than mystical powers barely explicable by theologians – the new enlightened judges and law administrators could and must once again – such as in the Medieval Low Countries – return to the role of arbiter between socio-economic forces beyond ordinary personal influence, instead of instigating, through fabricated demonology and horrendous persecutions, mutual suspicion and waning solidarity among the commoners. Hence, with the end of the witch hunts the European states reached maturity, as it were, if only by way of trickery. It had achieved a new political basis in the burghers and the emerging *bourgeoisie*, and a new ideology in the form of *mercantilism* – but one of the most significant long term effects of the trickery was recurring starvation and famine in many parts of Europe well into the 19th century. State monopolies had spoilt the age old free flow of surplus staple products along well established trade routes which characterized the heyday of the Hanseatic League in the 14th and 15th centuries – and it was, moreover, these monopolies which were attacked by the Enlightenment philosophers, with their ethically laden notions of *laissez faire* from in mid 18th century.

Towards the end of the preceding "state consolidation century", with the highly tense social matrix between a jealous nobility, a bewildered clergy, "up and coming" peasantry and yeomanry, and an unpredictable *bourgeoisie*, it would certainly have been exceedingly counterproductive, and even hazardous, for the respective European states to proceed with witch persecutions. And the fading away of these persecutions started already by the mid 17th century with the public activities of scientifically oriented burghers, who ridiculed the very *belief* in witchcraft, elucidating its inherently non-progressive character – and at the same time showed some scientific interest in the herbal usages practiced among those most unfortunate sacrificial lambs in the consolidation processes of the modern state.

Notes:

[1] See George H. Williams: *The Radical Reformation* (Weidenfeld & Nicolson, London, 1962).

[2] According to Rune Blix Hagen, in his *Dei europeiske trolldomsprosessane* (Samlaget, Oslo, 2007).

[3] Murray Bookchin: *The Third Revolution*, bd. I (Cassell, London, 1996), p. 42.

[4] A. F. Pollard i A. W. Ward, et. al.: *The Cambridge Modern History. Vol. II; The Reformation* (Macmillan, London, 1904), p. 183.

[5] For a detailed account of this phenomenon in Scandinavian history, see Halvdan Koht's *Norsk Bondereising* (Pax Forlag, Oslo, n. D.).

[6] This aspect has been emphasized by e. g. A. W. Ward, et. al., *op. cit.*, p. 184.

[7] Perez Zagorin: *Rebels and Rulers, 1500-1660; Vol. I; Society, States and Early Modern Revolution. Agrarian and Urban Rebellions* (Cambridge University Press, London, 1982).

[8] This dynamic is analyzed by Henri Pirenne in his *Early Democracies in the Low Countries*.

[9] Wallace Notestein: *A History of Witchcraft in England; From 1558 to 1718* (The American Historical Association, Washington, 1911), p. 297.

[10] Notestein, *op. cit.*, ch. XII, "Glanville and Webster and the Literary War over Witchcraft."

[11] For a discussion of Norwegian peasant revolts from te Reformation to the Age of Democratic Revolution, see P.

M. Makhno: *Crown Whims and Farmers' Endurance; Miitarization, Over-Taxation and Farmers' Resistance in Denmark-Norway, 1500-1800* (Nisus Publishing, Ulefoss, 2013). E-book available from Barnes & Noble.

[12] Palmer, Colton and Kramer: *A History of the Modern World* (McGraw Hill, London, 2007), p. 149.

[13] Christina Larner: *Enemies of God* (Chatto and Windus, London, 1981).

[14] An overview of the ideological diversity with respect to the witch hunts, see Rune Blix Hagen: *op. cit.*

[15] Palmer, Colton and Kramer: *op. cit.*, p. 227.

[16] For a brief but informative overview, see Blix Hagen: *op. cit.*

[17] The opening line in Bodin's *Demomanie des Sorciers*, quoted by Rev. Alphonses Joseph-Mary August Montague Summers, who believed fully in the evils of witch craft, in his *The History of Witchcraft* (The Mystic Press, London, n. D.), p. 1. Summers, for his part, compared the witch with "a heretic and an anarchist."

[18] Discussed in Notestein: *op. cit.*, ch. VII and XII.

[19] These oscillations may be seen from the judicial registers from the most relevant regions of the actual time period, presented by Gunnar W. Knutsen in his

"Trolldomsprosessene på Østlandet; en kulturhistorisk undersøkelse," in *Tingbokprosjektet*, Oslo, 1998.

[20] Sølvi Sogner: *Trolldomsprosessene i Norge på 1500-1600-tallet* (Oslo, 1981).

[21] Palmer, Colton and Kramer: *op. cit.*

[22] Palmer, Colton and Kramer: *op. cit.*, p. 239.

[22] Notestein: *op. cit.*, p. 284.

Printed in Great Britain
by Amazon